Faithful Heart

Author: K. Lee

KLEPub.com

Copyright:

Published by Krystal Lee Enterprises (KLE Publishing) Copyright © 2022 by K. Lee All rights reserved. Please send comments and questions:
Krystal Lee Enterprises
services@KLEPub.com
sales@KLEPub.com
To Reach the Author:
Email: info@authorklee.com
Web: AuthorKLee.com Social Media: @AuthorKLee 770-240-0089 Ext. 1
Printed in the United States of America.

All rights reserved. No part of this book may be reproduced or transmitted in any form or by any means, electronic or mechanical, including photocopying, recording or any information storage and retrieval system without written permission of the publisher except for brief quotations used in reviews, written specifically for inclusion in a newspaper, blog, magazine, or academic paper.
ISBN: 978-1-945066-15-3

In Loving Dedication

To the many living with faithful hearts and betraying minds that forget your memories. Know you are loved and even when it gets tough, you are still not alone. You have a tribe you know and don't know praying for you. But most importantly, You have a God in Heaven that still calls you son or daughter. You are loved and very much. Shalom...

Special Thanks to my friend Beverly Danner, my beautiful Aunt Monica Laing, my cherished Cousin Wendy Campbell, and my beloved Grandma Sandra Lucas xoxox.

Sitting here looking out the window. I have not committed a crime besides getting old. I feel like the prisoner being held within my body sheltered away from the world and those I love.

I miss home. I miss family. I miss my old life. Looking out the window reminds me I am not as free as a bird.

When I was free, I used to rip and run and be all over town. I had a loving husband who partnered with me in life and two children that I loved dearly.

The grandchildren were aplenty. The joys, the laughs, the correction, even the fights and arguments I miss.

Now it is so weird for my room to be so silent. The most I hear is the groans of the woman who lay in her bed next to me.

How did my room grow so still? How did time seem to be frozen still? I rarely see a mirror so I don't know the image of my face to track the days. I wonder about my hair.

I loved a short haircut that essentiated my oval face. I remember my appointments were every two weeks like clockwork.

Now, the only thing that seems to be on schedule is the clock ticking forward.

My family is close, but yet so far. I feel guilty that I don't remember and the only thing real to me are my feelings.

I feel love, afraid, anger, shame, joy, but also pain. I want to remember, but I don't.

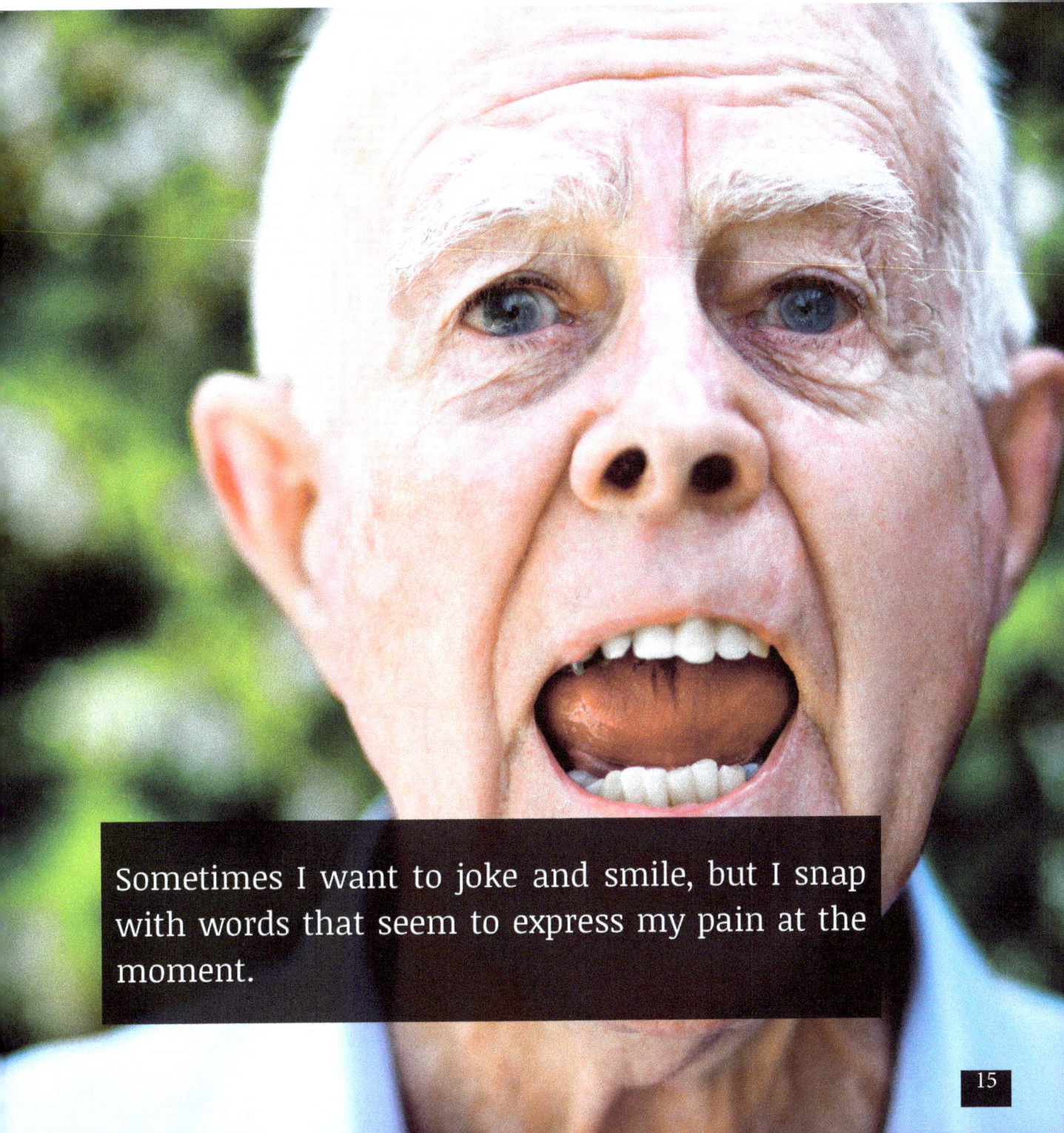

Sometimes I want to joke and smile, but I snap with words that seem to express my pain at the moment.

I still want the laughs, the looks that say I love you and not feel sorry for you. I don't want pity, I want love. I want to know I am loved and cared for by the God above. I know it is a tall order.

No, I am not perfect, but isn't life filled with imperfect people? Must I suffer now for my sins when I was younger? Or can I too live and love again? Is God only for the young, babies, and those that are strong?

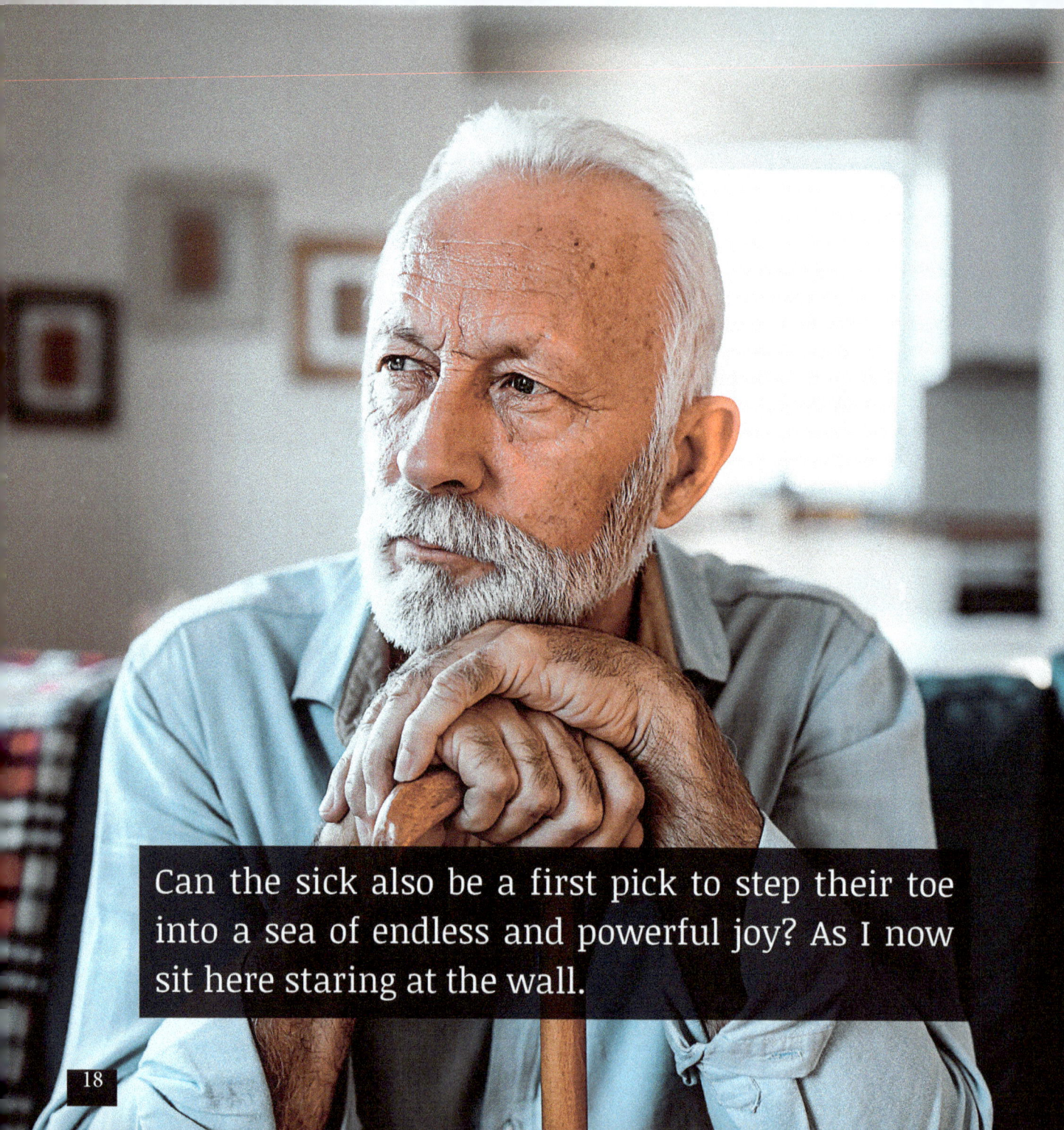

Can the sick also be a first pick to step their toe into a sea of endless and powerful joy? As I now sit here staring at the wall.

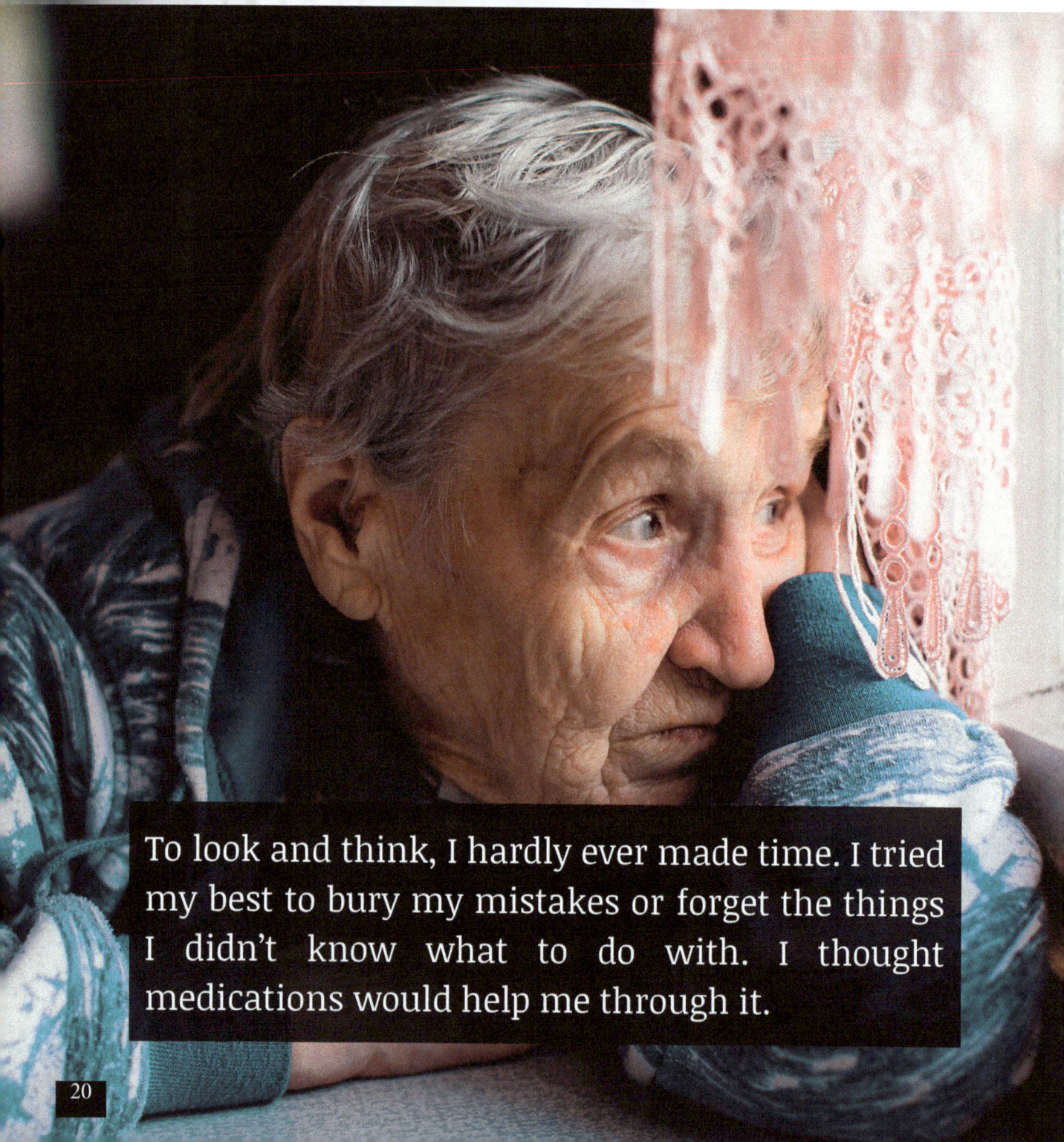

To look and think, I hardly ever made time. I tried my best to bury my mistakes or forget the things I didn't know what to do with. I thought medications would help me through it.

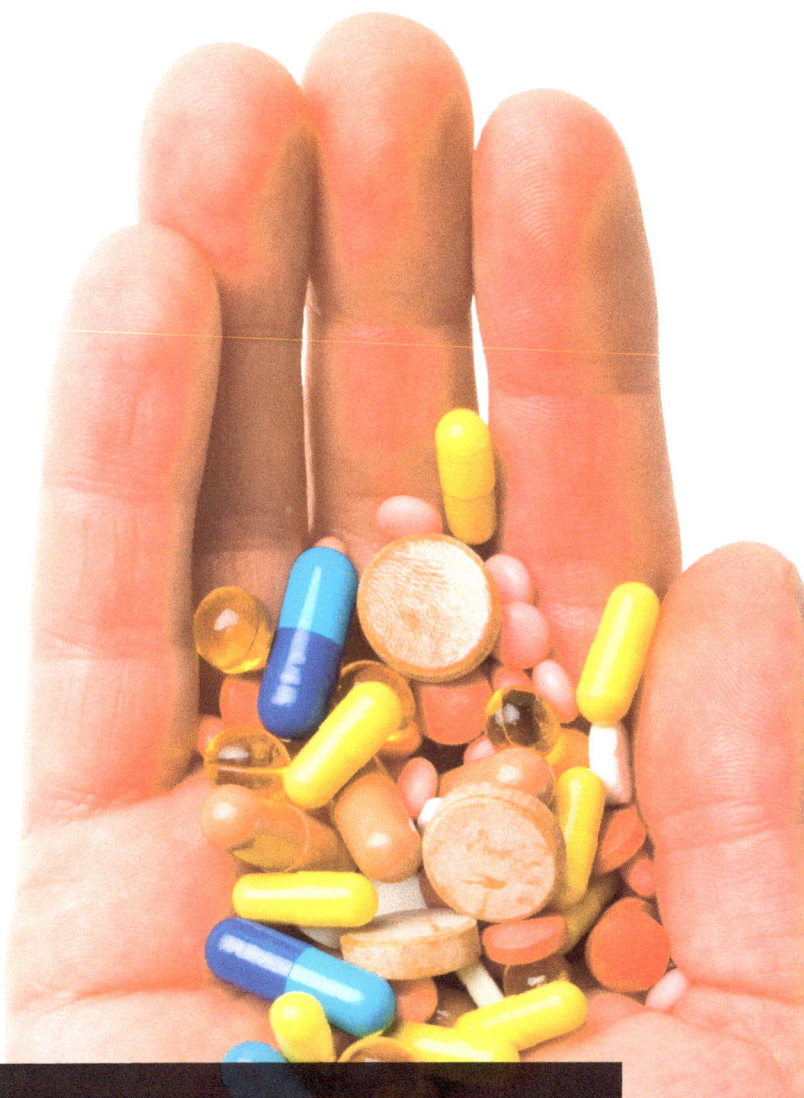

Now it seems like I take pills like eating a bag of candies, it is so surreal. I pray and call on a name I always knew, to show me the way. To send me a sign that would be my miracle.

Then one day you came! You are not a stranger, in fact, I know you all too well. You are my angel whom I have known all your life.

I remember the many summers you came and filled my house with cheer. I remember the pool table top that you ruined with your melted orange popsicle.

I can see your face as you cried, not because you were in trouble, but because you disappointed me. I remember your gentle spirit and how you always loved me.

I remember our chats when I would ask have you eaten and you couldn't remember. Funny now, you ask me, and I too don't remember. Your smile brings back memories that play in my mind and my heart.

I don't know the names of your little ones but they light up my room. To see them reminds me of how important you have been and people like you to those who sit and look out the window.

For those that sit in their bed and stare at a tv. For those that sit in the silence, the dark, and yearn to hear a laugh. I may not remember seeing you with my eyes, but my heart remembers every visit.

Jeremiah 17:9-10

"The heart is deceitful above all things, And desperately wicked; Who can know it? I, the LORD, search the heart, I test the mind, Even to give every man according to his ways, According to the fruit of his doings."

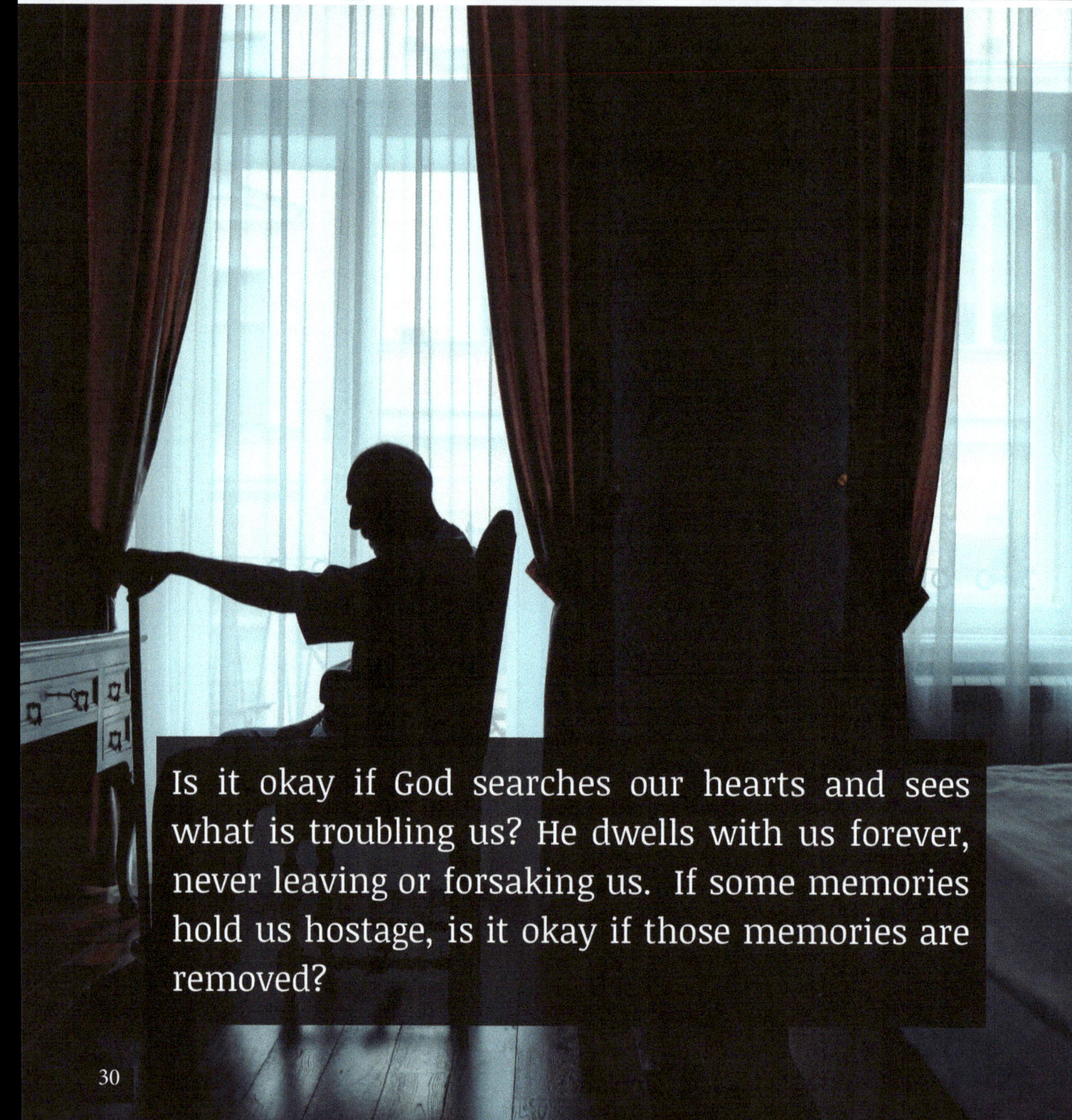

Is it okay if God searches our hearts and sees what is troubling us? He dwells with us forever, never leaving or forsaking us. If some memories hold us hostage, is it okay if those memories are removed?

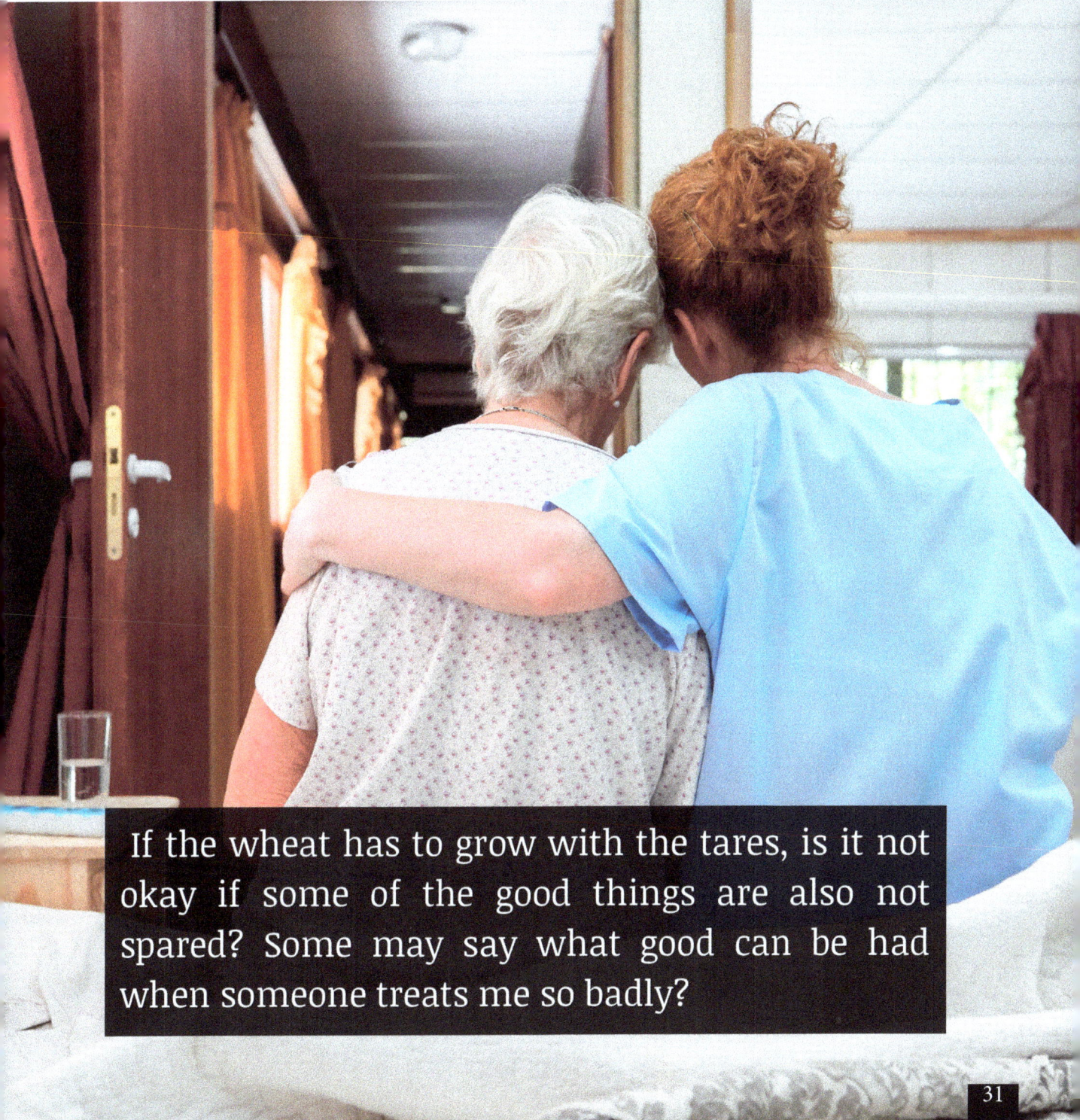

If the wheat has to grow with the tares, is it not okay if some of the good things are also not spared? Some may say what good can be had when someone treats me so badly?

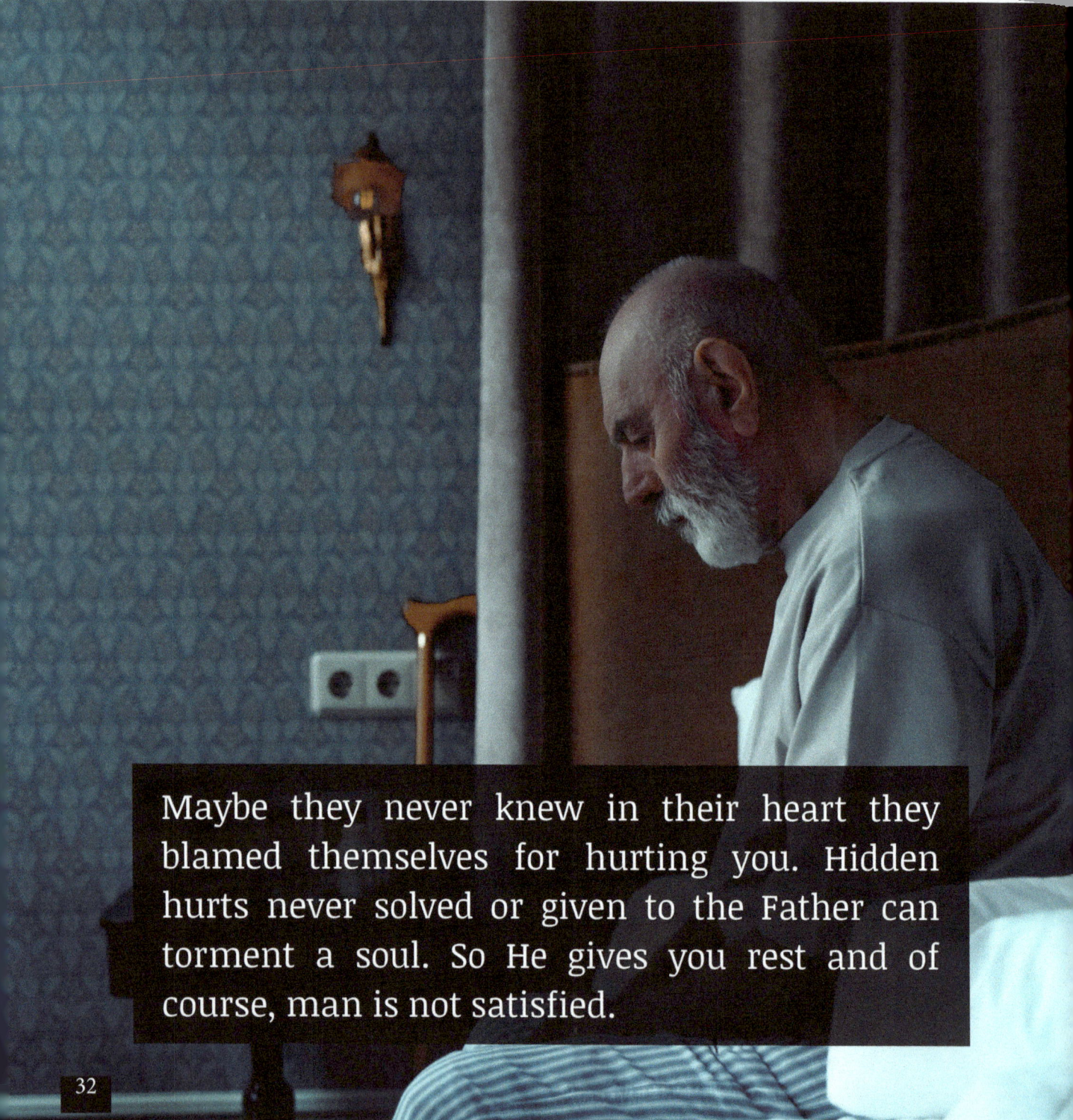

Maybe they never knew in their heart they blamed themselves for hurting you. Hidden hurts never solved or given to the Father can torment a soul. So He gives you rest and of course, man is not satisfied.

Proverbs 27:20 says Hell and destruction are never satisfied.

When I had my memories I wanted to forget, but now not having them I am angry they are gone.

Why do I not do what I want to do, but do what I don't want to do?

I want to love and be loved. At times I know that is not what I do. Although you may not see it or feel it at times, trust that it is still there.

I am still me even though I cannot see my past as clearly as you. I beg of you mercy and grace to endure this phase of my life. This too shall pass some day...

I cannot explain it, but my faithful heart feels it. Looking out the window and seeing your face in my heart's memory, I see my reason for being. I think silently to myself about what matters now.

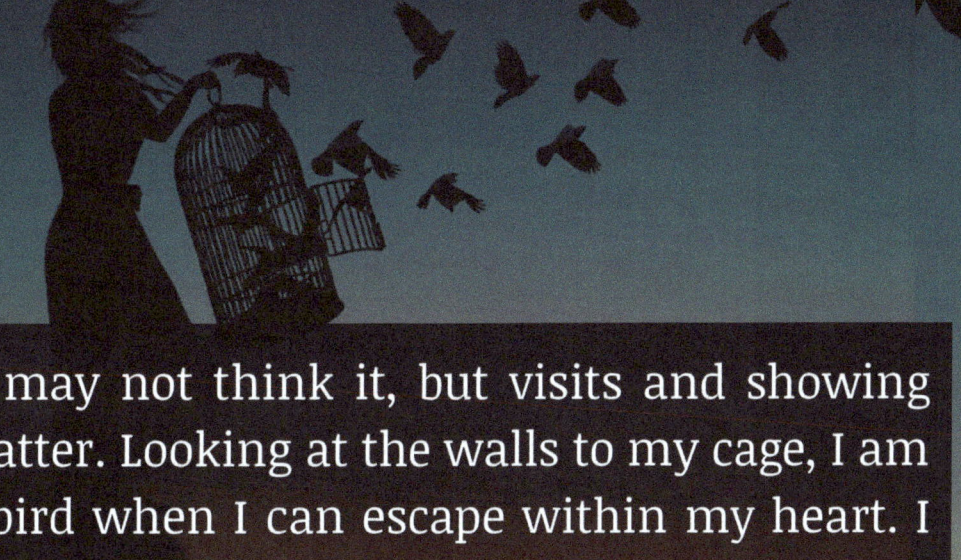

People may not think it, but visits and showing love matter. Looking at the walls to my cage, I am a free bird when I can escape within my heart. I can enjoy my world when I have your love filling it.

Something happens to a person when a little one takes you to a place where life began. Oh, how I love children and grandchildren.

Seeing them, feeling their little hands, and knowing that I won't be forgotten matters.

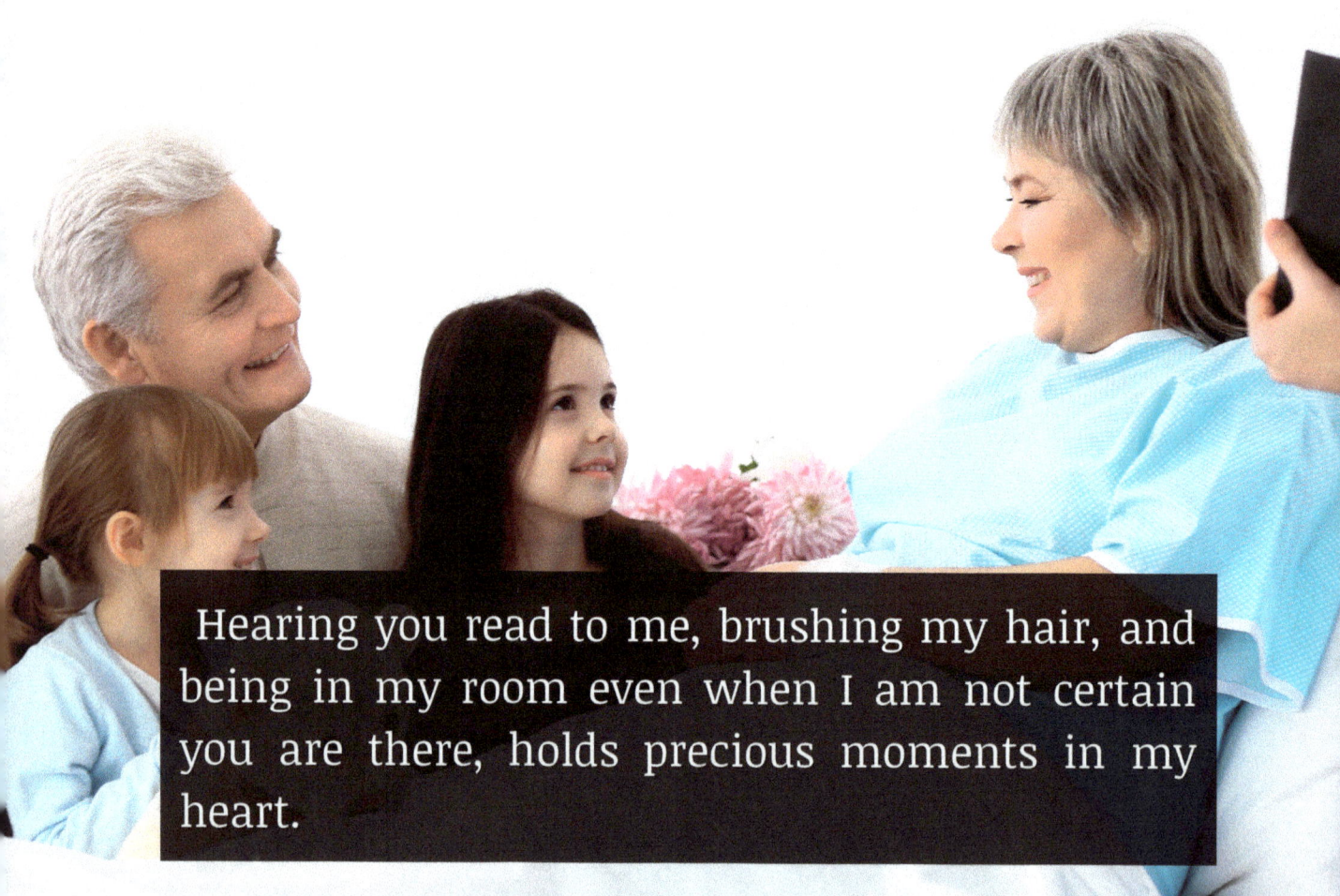

Hearing you read to me, brushing my hair, and being in my room even when I am not certain you are there, holds precious moments in my heart.

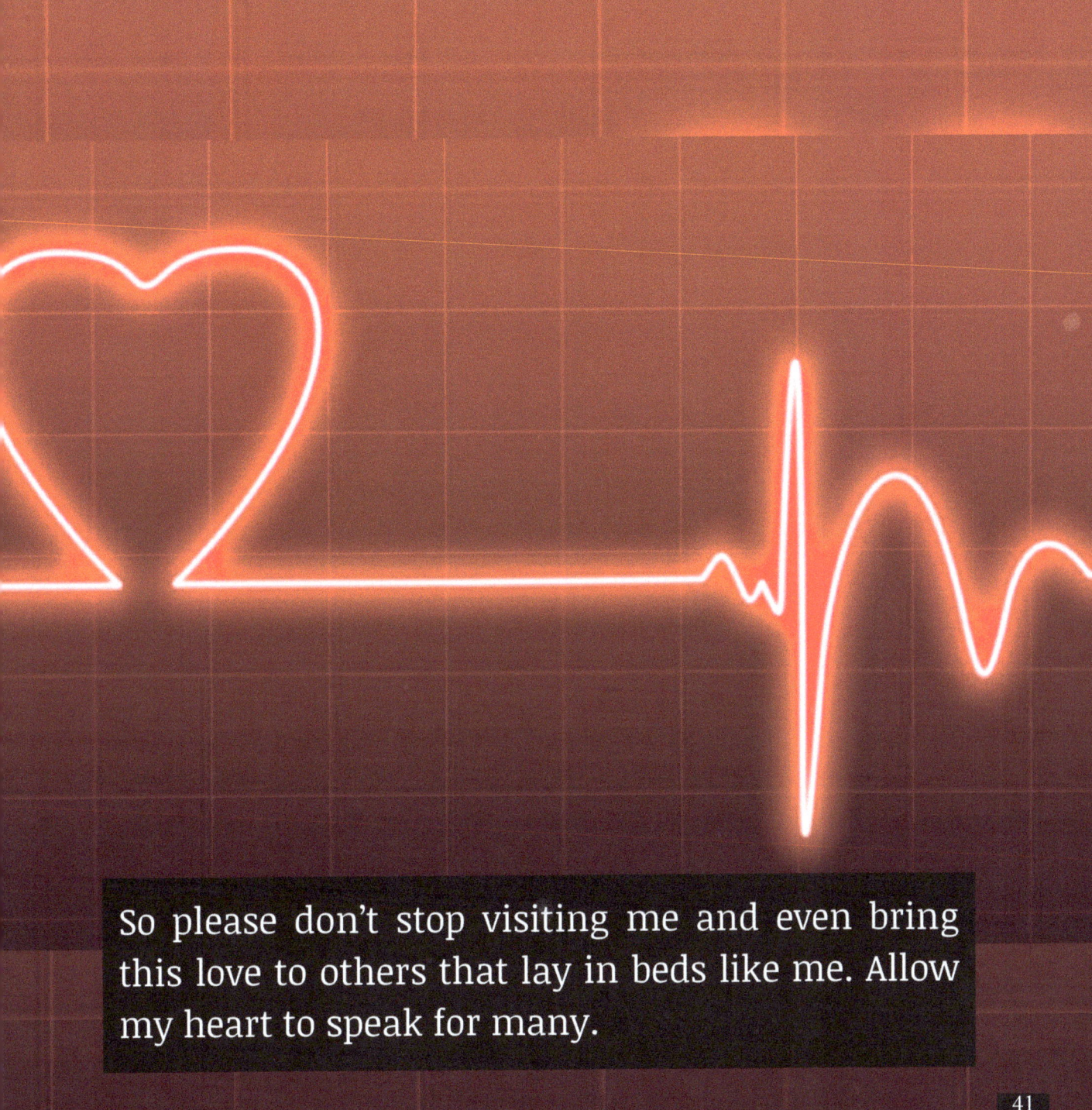

So please don't stop visiting me and even bring this love to others that lay in beds like me. Allow my heart to speak for many.

Allow me to share, no one deserves to be here. Deserves to be lost in their own thoughts or feeling worlds a part. I am blessed that I have many that come and visit to see about me.

I pray for those who don't. To have a better memory and recall those you gave your life for, nursed, healed, or fed, that now have no time for you can leave you dead inside.

Luke 17:14-19

And as they went they were cleansed. 15 Then one of them, when he saw that he was healed, turned back, praising God with a loud voice; 16 and he fell on his face at Jesus' feet, giving him thanks. Now he was a Samaritan. 17 Then Jesus answered, "Were not ten cleansed? Where are the nine? 18 Was no one found to return and give praise to God except this foreigner?" 19 And he said to him, "Rise and go your way; your faith has made you well."

Take courage, if people who were decaying on the inside could not take a moment to thank the one that healed them from death, it is no wonder that some do not make time to thank you for life.

Yet, there was one that was faithful that returned. There are many people that I learned care for me and not all of them are family.

Sure there are nurses here for money only, but then there are so many that I feel love me. I don't know their names but I feel their smile and pleasant demeanor wrap its arms around me.

Thank you to the many that have come but I don't remember.

I know people cannot live each day with me here, there, or anywhere. We all know that certain conditions make living at home impossible.

I just want to speak for the many that may not have the words to tell you. Our hearts feel you. Our minds at rest see you.

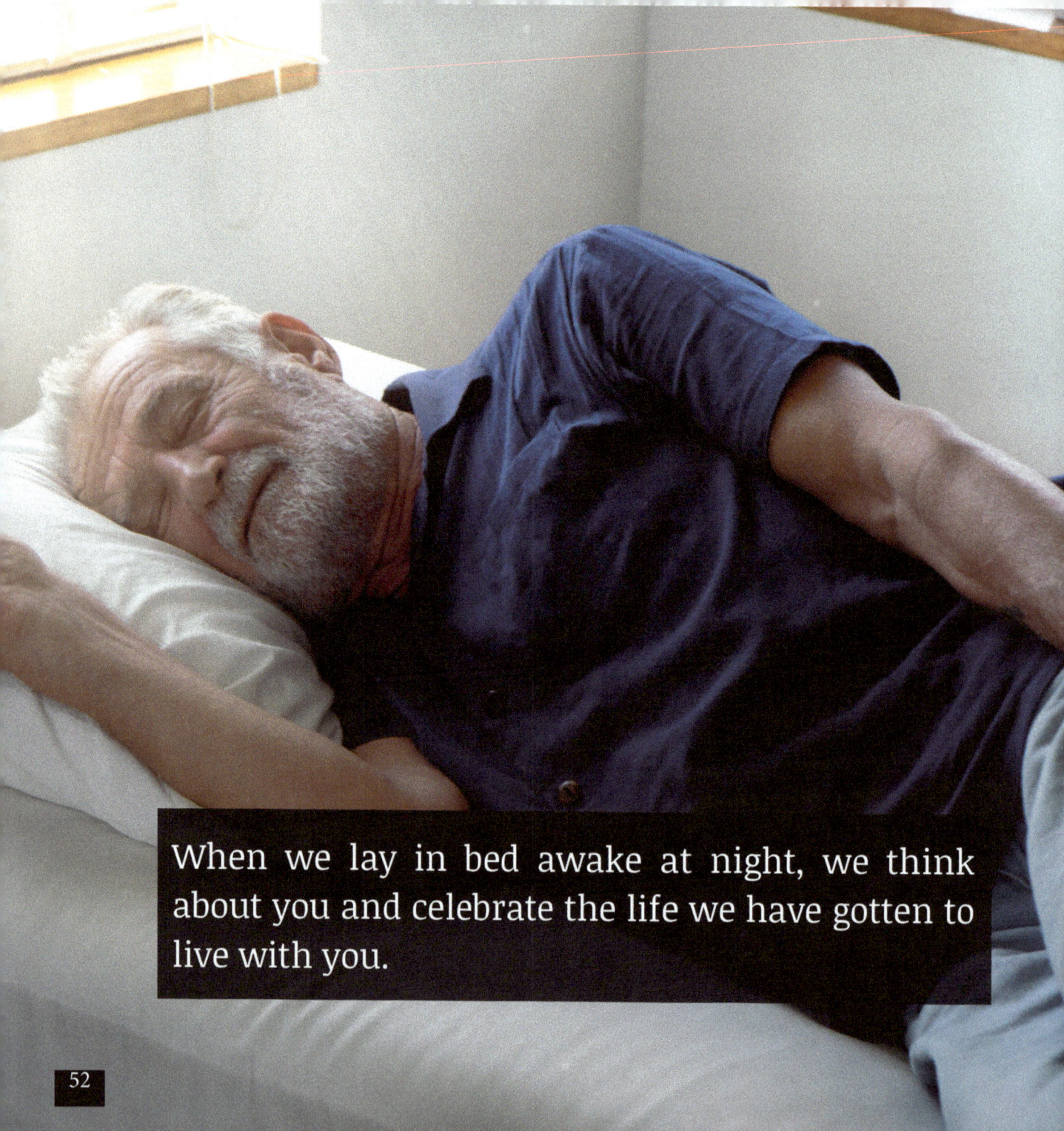

When we lay in bed awake at night, we think about you and celebrate the life we have gotten to live with you.

We rejoice inwardly to see your face and know that we have a place in your life. Some roads we walk alone, in our thoughts, but we are not alone, are we?

You are special, and you are the miracle we long to see. Your appearance reminds us God has not forgot. Your coming reminds us, imperfect people can be loved.

Your care shows us that we matter and we are still able to serve in God's master plan even until our last day. No one here is perfect. We all hold regrets, but we never once regretted loving you!

Don't Forget!

So please don't forget about me and visit me as often as you can.

Tell me about your journeys because for a moment I can see them with you. I get a new wind of life when you come around. You fill my heart with the noise I don't immediately see.

You fill my heart with the joy I don't get from the tv. You fill my heart with laughter that I don't get from staring at the clock or watching the walls.

You are the light, that shines in a dark room. You are the reason I don't go into the light before my time.

I hold on, because the Love God shows to me through you, tears up any plans for depression, regret, or heartache.

I am free as a bird, even though I sit in this room because I know God loves me because He sent me you.

He sent your arms to hold me. Your voice to comfort me. Your hugs to warm my soul.

Everything you do for those who are God's children you have done for our Lord and Savior Yeshua (Jesus) Christ our King.

Matthew 25:34-36

35 For I was hungry and you gave me food, I was thirsty and you gave me drink, I was a stranger and you welcomed me, 36 I was naked and you clothed me, I was sick and you visited me, I was in prison and you came to me.'

Matthew 25:37-39

37 Then the righteous will answer him, saying, 'Lord, when did we see you hungry and feed you, or thirsty and give you drink? **38** And when did we see you a stranger and welcome you, or naked and clothe you? **39** And when did we see you sick or in prison and visit you?'

Matthew 25:40

40 And the King will answer them, 'Truly, I say to you, as you did it to one of the least of these you did it to me.'

In all that you do, always remember I am proud and so grateful for you. All that you have done and continue to do, is locked into my heart and will never depart.

My mind betrays me, but my heart is faithful. Whatever you do, please don't forget to visit me as often as you can. Thank you for being a beacon that God can live through.

Order More Books Today!

If you need a ghostwriter, editor, or want to publish a book visit **KLEPub.com** or call **770-240-0089 Ext. 1**

Checkout Our Latest New Titles
KLEPub.com

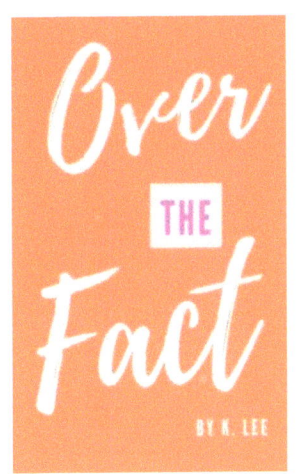
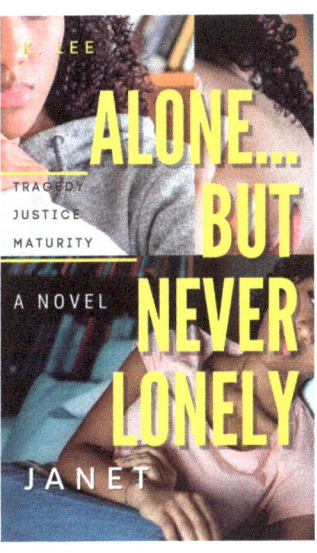

Author

BWCCLOTHINGSTORE.COM

K. Lee

Is a mother of 4 beautiful children. Writing books, plays, and films she enjoys very much, but what she loves most is coaching and preaching. Giving back to people who need hope, love, and a friendly reminder people are not alone is her life's passion. She is the author of the Youth Personal Development series The Lesson, a ghostwriter, life coach, ordained clergy, and entrepreneur. To learn more and connect with her visit AuthorKLee.com and connect on Social Media @ Authorklee on all platforms FB, IG, TikTok, YouTube, and Twitter.

To my beautiful Grandmother Lucas, I love you ! Thank you for reminding me of what matters in this life and the one to come. You are a jewel imperfectly perfect and I love you!

www.ingramcontent.com/pod-product-compliance
Lightning Source LLC
Chambersburg PA
CBHW051359110526
44592CB00023B/2889